PRESENTATION SUCCESS

A Step-by-Step Approach

Jackie L. Jankovich Hartman
Elaine A. LeMay

Presentation Success – A Step-by-Step Approach by Jackie L. Jankovich Hartman and Elaine A. LeMay

Vice President/Publisher: Dave Shaut
Acquisitions Editor: Pamela Person
Developmental Editor: Taney Wilkins
Marketing Manager: Rob Bloom
Production Editor: Margaret M. Bril
Manufacturing Coordinator: Sandee Milewski
Production House: Cover to Cover Publishing, Inc.
Printer: Webcom Limited

Printed in Canada
1 2 3 4 5   03 02 01 00

For more information contact South-Western, 5101 Madison Road, Cincinnati, Ohio, 45227 or find us on the Internet at http://www.swcollege.com
For permission to use material from this text or product, contact us by
• telephone: 1-800-730-2214
• fax: 1-800-730-2215
• web: http://www.thomsonrights.com

Library of Congress Cataloging-in-Publication Data
Jankovich Hartman, Jackie L.
    Presentation success : a step-by-step approach / Jackie L. Jankovich Hartman, Elaine A. LeMay.
        p. cm.
    ISBN 0-324-10092-2
    1. Business presentations. I. Title: Effective presentations. II. LeMay, Elaine A. III. Title.

HF5718.22 .J36 2000
808.5'1--dc21
                                                                00-056328

This book is printed on acid-free paper.

ABOUT THE AUTHORS

Jackie Jankovich Hartman, Ph.D., is an Assistant Professor in the College of Business at Colorado State University where she specializes in management and organizational communication. Jackie's works are published in *Academy of Business Administration, Academy of Human Resource Development, Business Communication Quarterly, Performance and Instruction* and *The Journal of Marketing Theory and Practice.* Jackie is a consultant for corporate and government clients and leads workshops in Organizational and Strategic Communication, Communication Styles, Organizational Protocol, Business Etiquette, Effective Presentations, and Human Resource Development.

Elaine LeMay, Ph.D., is an Instructor in the College of Business at Colorado State University where she teaches Business Communication, Management, and Human Resource Management classes. Elaine has over 20 years of experience both working for and consulting with organizations. Her areas of expertise include Self-Managed Work Teams, Organizational Assessments, Communication Audits, Managing Change, Performance Management, Effective Hiring, and Communication Styles. Her clients include high tech, health care, manufacturing, and insurance organizations as well as city and federal government agencies.

PREFACE

One presentation can make or break a career! This sounds harsh but the reality is first impressions count, and first impressions are often based on communication skills. Organizational leaders invariably cite effective communication skills as one of the top three most important requirements for organizational and personal success. Therefore, delivering effective presentations is one of the fundamental components of being a successful communicator, and thus the skills are worth acquiring early and improving steadily.

As a result of our work with business people and students, we were inspired to alleviate the fears and stresses of those preparing to make presentations. Therefore, this book was written to provide you with all you need to know to deliver a high-quality, professional, and memorable presentation. This book provides a step-by-step, systematic approach that will guide you from start to finish when developing and delivering a presentation. The book is a complete source for the novice presenter and it will provide unique pointers for experienced presenters.

The book is organized into four phases. Each phase consists of building blocks that will lead you to success when making presentations. By using the checklists provided throughout the book you will avoid common mistakes made by others as well as eliminate frantic moments and memorable disasters.

The guidelines discussed in this book are tried and true—they really work! Implement these guidelines and you will become the powerful and successful communicator necessary in today's work environment.

TABLE OF CONTENTS

TABLE OF CHECKLISTS

INTRODUCTION

Published reports cite that the single greatest fear of men and women is the fear of speaking in public. Not death, not taxes, not even driving in New York City are as intimidating as speaking in front of others. And yet public speaking is a necessary and everyday occurrence for people in the workplace.

The importance and value of verbal communication skills in business is increasing, and the standards are rising. Many executives now list communication skills as a prime requisite for hiring and promotability. Multiple studies have reported that when organizations have been surveyed about skill shortages, verbal communication skills are the most lacking ability in their applicant pool. Effective presentation skills are a critical component of the verbal communication skills category. Therefore, developing effective presentation skills is crucial to the success of your career.

Effective public speaking is a skill that can be developed and improved. This book presents guidelines to help you generate an effective business presentation. These guidelines are divided into four phases.

Phase One: Organizing the Presentation

Phase Two: Developing the Content

Phase Three: Creating and Using Visual Aids

Phase Four: Delivering the Presentation

Each phase consists of building blocks that will lay the groundwork for a systematic approach designed to help you develop your presentation.

PHASE ONE:
ORGANIZING THE PRESENTATION

The first phase when constructing a presentation is **Organizing the Presentation**. This phase includes three building blocks.

1 **Defining the Purpose**

1 2 **Analyzing the Audience**

1 2 3 **Choosing the Organizational Plan**

◻1 *Defining the Purpose*

The general purpose of most business presentations falls into at least one of three categories:

- ❑ To Inform
- ❑ To Persuade
- ❑ To Recommend

You should expand the *general purpose* by including the **specific purpose**. This process is similar to defining the topic of a written message. Effective presenters are able to define the purpose of their presentation in one sentence and relate it to their audience's needs. Presenters who are unable to articulate their purpose when planning a presentation have difficulty conveying this purpose to an audience.

For example, when presenting, your general and specific purpose might be:

- ❑ To *inform* employees about a **new healthcare provider.**

- ❑ To *persuade* management to **increase the research and development budget.**

- ❑ To *recommend* that the company **reimburse employee's tuition costs.**

When presenters are unable to convey the purpose of their presentation to the audience, an ineffective presentation results.

The general and specific purpose will drive your presentation. All of the supporting information that you will include must fall within the framework that you have built by defining your purpose. A well-defined purpose will help you to determine the information you should include and that which you should discard. Building Block #1,

| 1 | **Defining the Purpose,**
is essential to the success of organizing your presentation as is Building Block #2, Analyzing the Audience.

1 2 | *Analyzing the Audience*

Analyzing the Audience enables you to structure your presentation to link your purpose with the audience's needs. Too often a presentation is based on the wrong perspective; speakers present what they want rather than considering the audience's needs. Your presentation should be customized for the audience, at the same time accomplishing your purpose.

By analyzing your audience, you will understand the participants' needs so that you can effectively develop and deliver the necessary material. To analyze your audience, ask yourself the following questions:

❑ **How many people will you address?**

If you are addressing a small group, under 10, it is easy to interact with them during the presentation. However, addressing over 10 people makes it more difficult to interact while presenting.

❑ **What are the names of the audience members?**

If possible, refer to the audience's members by name. Arrive at the meeting place early. Introduce yourself to the audience members as they arrive in order to establish a rapport before the presentation begins. As the presenter, you will feel comfortable addressing friendly faces, and the audience will respond warmly to someone they have already met.

❑ What is the cultural diversity of the audience?

Determine the demographic constitution of your audience. Anticipate whether gender, age, ethnic, and/or cultural differences and/or sensitivities exist and whether these differences and sensitivities will impact your presentation. In addition, be aware of the primary and secondary languages spoken by the audience members. If you are speaking a language that is secondary to your audience members, decrease your speaking rate and use common words. Also, consider using additional visuals to supplement the verbal portion of your presentation. Furthermore, consider entertaining questions throughout the presentation rather than only at the end of your presentation.

❑ What is the composition or job diversity of the audience?

Relate your message to the group's functions and responsibilities. If the audience is homogeneous, target their specific needs. However, if the audience is diverse, target the needs common to all.

❑ What is your audience's attitude about you, the presenter?

Has your audience had positive or negative interaction with you in the past? If so, this attitude, whether it be positive or negative, might bias your audience and affect the presentation. If the audience's attitude is negative, open your presentation with neutral news or state a commonality. This approach will allow the audience to agree with you and be more receptive to the rest of your presentation.

❑ **What is your audience's attitude about the topic?**

Are you presenting neutral or good news? If so, your audience will probably be receptive and open-minded. Or, are you presenting controversial or negative news? If so, be prepared—your audience might be close-minded or argumentative. If indeed your audience might react negatively, spend more time researching their needs. Also, allocate more time establishing your credibility in the introduction of your presentation. It is essential when analyzing your audience to consider an audience's probable reaction to your message.

❑ **How much does your audience know about the subject? What is the audience's level of knowledge about the subject?**

Avoid boring audiences with material that is common knowledge. Determine the audience's level of understanding and needs. For example, a presentation prepared for technical first-line managers might be significantly different than a presentation prepared for the board of directors. The technical managers might be more interested in the specifics of how you arrived at the bottom line, whereas the board of directors might only be interested in the bottom line.

❑ **What is the presentation environment? Is it formal or informal?**

If the environment is formal, consider maintaining control of the presentation and follow with a question-and-answer session. However, if the presentation is informal, consider conducting an interactive presentation allowing audience interaction. When possible, move towards the audience rather than remaining fixed behind a podium; you, as the presenter, will then seem more accessible to the audience.

The time spent researching your audience is invaluable. A complete audience analysis will lead to a presentation that will accomplish its purpose and avoid a generic, impersonal presentation. Use the

Audience Analysis Checklist on page 20 to guide you when analyzing your audience.

Once you have spent time

1 **Defining the Purpose**
and

1 2 **Analyzing the Audience,**
it is time to assemble Building Block #3, Choosing the Organizational Plan.

1 2 3 *Choosing the Organizational Plan*

There are three sections to any presentation: **The Introduction, the Body,** and **the Conclusion.**

The Introduction section includes a greeting and an agenda for the presentation.

The Body section includes the details or supporting information needed to help the audience understand the presentation and its purpose.

The Conclusion section includes the evaluations, recommendations, and/or actions desired.

As a presenter, you should determine the order of these three sections based on the purpose of your presentation and the audience's needs. The order in which you present these three sections is nearly as important as the information itself.

As a presenter, you can benefit from using the psychological factor of order. You can establish order by determining the appropriate organizational plan. You have two options available to you when choosing the correct organizational plan—the indirect plan and the direct plan.

Indirect Organizational Plan

Most people are familiar with organizing a presentation using the indirect plan. The Introduction is followed by the Body, which is then followed by the Conclusion. The details, or the supporting information contained in the Body section, lead the audience to understand the information in the Conclusion.

I.   The Introduction Section

II.   The Body Section

III.   The Conclusion Section

The Indirect Plan is used when the audience needs the supporting information first, before they hear the conclusion or end result. The Indirect Plan is preferred when the audience might feel neutral or negative if they heard the conclusion before hearing the supporting information. Presenting the supporting information first justifies the evaluations, recommendations, and/or actions desired that you will make in the conclusion section. When your purpose is to present negative or sensitive news, the supporting information will lead your audience to better understand and hopefully accept this information before it is presented. If you anticipate that your audience will resist part of the information, do not state this information at the beginning of the presentation. As a presenter you should always consider the ways in which the audience will react to your presentation.

The following outlines illustrate the use of the indirect organizational plan when your purpose is to inform, make recommendations to, or persuade an audience.

Indirect Informative Outline

I.   The Introduction Section

II.   The Body Section:
Fact
Fact
Fact

III.   The Conclusion Section:
Evaluation

Indirect Recommendation Outline

I.   The Introduction Section

II.   The Body Section:
Proof
Proof
Proof

III.   The Conclusion Section:
Recommendation

Indirect Persuasive Outline

I. The Introduction Section

II. The Body Section:
Reason
Reason
Reason

III. The Conclusion Section:
Action Desired

The following, more-developed outlines illustrate the use of the Indirect Plan when delivering neutral, negative, and persuasive messages.

Indirect Informative Presentation Example:

General and Specific Purpose—To *inform* employees of a new healthcare provider.

I.   The Introduction: Discussion of the company's new healthcare provider.

II. The Body (supporting information):
  - Who is the healthcare provider
  - What will they provide
  - When will the new provider take over
  - Why are we changing healthcare providers

III. The Conclusion (evaluation):
  - The change in healthcare providers will improve the employees' medical care.

Indirect Negative News Presentation Example:

General and Specific Purpose—To *inform* board of directors of the **division's financial status.**

I.   The Introduction: Presentation of the division's financial status.

II.   The Body (supporting information):
   - Division's goals
   - Division's strategy to achieve goals
   - Increased competition
   - Decrease in market share
   - Union strike

III. The Conclusion (negative news):
   - The division's profit decreased 10 percent.

Indirect Persuasive Presentation Example:

General and Specific Purpose—To *persuade* management to **increase the research and development budget.**

I.   The Introduction: Discussion of the research and development budget.

II. The Body (supporting information):
- Current budget
- Current projects
- Competitor's spending
- Proposed projects
- Proposed budget increase
- Profitable projects

III. The Conclusion (action desired):
- Increase research and development budget by "x" amount.

As a result of using the Indirect Plan, the audience will better accept a change, negative news, or sensitive news. Remember that your audience's reaction should be considered when choosing the organizational plan. The second organizational plan you can use is the Direct Plan.

Direct Organizational Plan

The Direct Plan reverses the order of the Indirect Plan and places the Conclusion before the Body section as illustrated below.

I.   The Introduction Section

II.   The Conclusion Section

III.   The Body Section

When your presentation will result in the audience feeling positive or when the information is analytical resulting in a complex presentation, use the Direct Plan. The Direct Plan places the Conclusion section, which contains an evaluation, recommendation, and/or action desired, first followed by the Body section, which contains the supporting information. The following outlines illustrate the use of the Direct Plan.

Direct Positive News Presentation

I.   The Introduction Section

II.   The Conclusion Section (evaluation, recommendation, and/or action desired):

III. The Body Section:
      Fact
      Fact
      Fact

Direct Analytical Presentation

I.   The Introduction Section

II.   The Conclusion Section (evaluation, recommendation, and/or action desired):

III. The Body Section:
      Fact/Analysis
      Fact/Analysis
      Fact/Analysis

When presenting information that will result in the audience feeling positive, use the Direct Plan. In addition, when the information you are presenting is complex and might cause confusion for the audience, use the Direct Plan. Remember, when using the Direct Plan, the sequence of the three sections is the Introduction, the Conclusion, and the Body.

The following, more-developed outlines illustrate the use of the Direct Plan when delivering positive news and analytical news. The difference between the two organizational plans, the indirect and direct, is the placement of the Conclusion section.

Direct Positive News Presentation Example:

General and Specific Purpose—To *inform* employees of an **improved company benefits package.**

   I.   The Introduction: Presentation of new company benefit.

   II.   The Conclusion (positive news): The new company benefit, a profit sharing plan, will allow all employees to share in the company's success.

   III.   The Body (supporting information):

- All employees are eligible
- Employees incur no costs
- Employees automatically share 10 percent of the profits
- New employee benefits package is effective this quarter

Direct Analytical News Example:

General and Specific Purpose—To *inform* the board of directors of **facility location options.**

I.   The Introduction: Discussion of facility location options.

II. The Conclusion (complex news): Recommendation of the proposed facility location site.

III. The Body (supporting information):
- Site One, advantages and disadvantages
- Site Two, advantages and disadvantages
- Sites One and Two compare and contrast

The guidelines just discussed indicate that when you present information that will result in the audience feeling neutral, uninterested, or negative, you should use the Indirect Plan. However, when presenting information that is positive or analytical, use the Direct Plan. It is important to understand that organizational plans are not set in stone. Some people will *always* prefer the Conclusion section first, even if negative news is being presented. Others will *always* prefer the Conclusion section at the end of the presentation, even if positive news is being presented. An effective audience analysis combined with the purpose and objectives of your presentation will help you choose the appropriate organizational plan.

Phase One: Organizing the Presentation Summary

Organizing your presentation is critical to the success of any business presentation. To effectively organize your presentation, Define the Purpose, Analyze the Audience, and Choose the Correct Organizational Plan. These three organizational building blocks provide a systematic approach that must be completed before you can move on to Phase Two: Developing the Content of your presentation.

Use the Organizing the Presentation Checklist on page 21 to guide you when organizing your presentation.

| 1 | *Defining the Purpose* |

| 1 2 | *Analyzing the Audience* |

| 1 2 3 | *Choosing the Organizational Plan* |

Phase One: Audience Analysis Checklist

- ☐ Determine how many people will attend the presentation.

- ☐ Analyze audience demographics.

- ☐ Consider the cultural sensitivity of the audience.

- ☐ Analyze why the members of the audience are present.

- ☐ Determine what the audience members have in common.

- ☐ Consider the attitudes of the audience prior to the presentation.

- ☐ Analyze the audience's reaction to you, the presenter.

- ☐ Determine what the audience already knows about the subject.

- ☐ Link the presentation purpose with the audience's needs.

- ☐ Determine the appropriate way to establish credibility with the audience.

- ☐ Determine the amount of background information the audience needs.

- ☐ Determine the information needed to satisfy the purpose of the presentation and the audience's needs.

- ☐ Determine the audience's understanding of technical terminology.

- ☐ Analyze the audience's possible reactions to the presentation.

Phase One: Organizing the Presentation Checklist

❑ Have you clearly defined your general and specific purpose in one sentence?

❑ Have you completed the audience analysis?

❑ Are you using the correct organizational plan—indirect or direct?

Phase One: Presentation Challenge

For each situation, determine the presentation's general and specific purpose, analyze the audience, and determine the correct organizational plan.

SITUATION ONE:

You have been assigned the role of department representative for the annual United Way Campaign. Your department is competing against other departments in your organization. You need to make a presentation to your colleagues generating enthusiasm for the competition.

General and Specific Purpose: _____

_____

_____

Audience Analysis: _____

_____

_____

Organizational Plan: _____

(continued)

Phase One: Presentation Challenge *(continued)*

SITUATION TWO:

As owner of a retail clothing store, you realize that the employee discount you offer does not compete with comparable stores. Make a presentation to your employees announcing the change from a 15 to 20 percent discount.

General and Specific Purpose: _____

_____

_____

_____

Audience Analysis: _____

_____

_____

_____

Organizational Plan: _____

(continued)

Phase One: Presentation Challenge *(continued)*

SITUATION THREE:

As owner of a retail clothing store, you realize that the employee discount you offer does not compete with comparable stores. However, you cannot afford to offer an increased discount to all employees. Make a presentation to your employees announcing the new discount policy. Employees working for the store less than one year will receive a 10 percent discount while those employed more than one year will receive a 20 percent discount.

General and Specific Purpose: _____

_____

_____

_____

Audience Analysis: _____

_____

_____

_____

Organizational Plan: _____

PHASE TWO:
DEVELOPING THE CONTENT

You have established why you are presenting (purpose), who you are addressing (audience), and the organizational plan you will use. The next phase in generating an effective presentation is **Developing the Content** of your presentation. You will develop the content of your presentation based on the general and specific purposes of the presentation, the audience attending, and the time you have been allotted. This phase, Developing the Content, must be completed before you can successfully deliver your presentation.

There are four building blocks to Phase Two: Developing the Content.

1 ***The Introduction***

1 2 ***The Body***

1 2 3 ***The Transitional Plan***

1 2 3 4 ***The Conclusion***

25

1 *The Introduction*

When introducing your presentation, you have approximately 60 seconds to catch your audience's attention and motivate them to listen to your presentation. To obtain your audience's attention, you need to answer two questions: "Why is this presentation important" and "What will I get out of this presentation." Answer these two questions in your introduction to establish credibility and build rapport with your audience.

Because your audience is most likely to remember what they hear first and last in a presentation, it is essential that you develop a strong introduction and closing.

Every introduction should include five introductory elements. These five elements are:

1. **Attention Getter**

2. **Background**

3. **Scope**

4. **Definition of Terms** (if necessary)

5. **The Plan of Presentation**

Attention Getter

Use an Attention Getter to attract the audience's attention and motivate them to listen to you. Choose an attention getter that relates to your audience as well as the subject matter and ties the two together.

For example:

❑ **Ask a question**

How many of you would like to double your sales revenue in the next 12 months?

❑ **Give an interesting statistic**

Do you realize that 50 percent of the homeless population have children under the age of 5?

❑ **State a rhetorical question or series of questions**

How many of you have ever taken a pencil home from work? How many of you have ever taken your stapler home to use for an evening? How many of you have stretched your lunch hour?

❑ **State a brief narrative**

In the old days, a manufacturer's attitude towards workers was, "Just do these tasks. You don't have to think." Managers at XYZ cannot survive using this outdated attitude.

❑ **State a familiar quotation (only if the author is known and respected by the audience)**

Ask not what your country can do for you, but what you can do for your country.

❑ **Discuss a commonality between yourself and the audience**

I know how lost I felt when I first started working here because there was no orientation program; how did you feel?

Your audience will listen intently to the first couple of sentences of your presentation; therefore, it is critical to carefully develop the opening of your presentation. Also, <u>make sure the Attention Getter relates to your purpose, topic, and audience.</u>

Background

The second introductory element you need to include is the Background. The Background <u>explains what happened in the past or what is happening now that makes your presentation important.</u> Your audience analysis will help you determine how much background you need to include in your presentation. If your audience is familiar with your topic, only a few background statements are necessary. On the other hand, you may need to further develop your background information if your audience is not familiar with your topic.

Background Example:

We are here today to discuss the implementation of a company orientation program. Research shows that those companies with formal orientation programs have lower turnover rates and higher morale. During the last three years our turnover rate has exceeded 18 percent, and the averages on the employee attitude survey have declined.

Scope

The third introductory element, the Scope, establishes the boundaries of your presentation. It explains <u>what is included and what is not included.</u>

Scope Example 1:

We are here to discuss gender discrimination. We are not going to address ethnic discrimination or age discrimination at this time.

Scope Example 2:

During the next 60 minutes, I will explain the advantages and disadvantages of an on-site daycare program, and I will profile how one successful daycare program is being used at Arbitron Corp. At this point, we are not going to discuss actual costs for this initiative.

The scope is similar to the Plan of Presentation, which will be discussed shortly, and many presenters will combine the two to eliminate redundancies.

Definition of Terms

The fourth introductory element is Definition of Terms. When analyzing your audience, determine what terms need to be defined or what technical jargon may be unfamiliar to the audience. When using unfamiliar terms throughout your presentation, define them in the introduction. If an unfamiliar term is used only once, define it when it is used.

> **Definition of Terms Example:**
>
> How many people would understand the following?
>
> 1. The H_2SO_4 content was so high that it created a hazardous condition (H_2SO_4 = sulfuric acid).
>
> 2. The golden handcuffs prevented Ms. Perez from leaving the company (Golden handcuffs = benefits that keep an employee from leaving a company).
>
> 3. The AG's office requested an update on the status of our investigation (AG = Attorney General).
>
> 4. EDI is the foundation of e-commerce (EDI = Electronic Data Interchange, which is computer-to-computer transmission of business information in a standard format).

The Plan of Presentation

The fifth introductory element, the Plan of Presentation, explains your presentation agenda and tells the audience what to expect. The agenda is essential; it previews your main ideas for the audience and creates continuity during the presentation, serving as a roadmap for your audience.

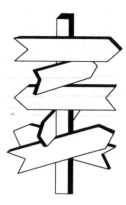

Below are two examples of a plan of presentation.

Plan of Presentation Example 1:

Today, we will discuss five ways to improve teamwork in our division.

Plan of Presentation Example 2:

This presentation will discuss the advantages and disadvantages of an employee orientation program, profile two different formats for an orientation program, and conclude with our recommendations.

The Plan of Presentation is the last of the five introductory elements. It should be the last thing you say in your introduction because it provides a smooth transition from the introduction itself to the body of your presentation.

To effectively organize your introduction it may be helpful to write out the information for each element of the introduction as shown in the following example.

Planning Your Introduction Example:

Purpose—To inform Carson Corporation executives on the advantages and disadvantages of implementing a corporate wellness program.

I. Introduction

    A. Attention Getter—Research shows that companies with effective wellness programs have reduced their medical care costs by 20 percent. How would you like our company to achieve these results?

    B. Background—Carson Corporation is spending an alarming amount on medical insurance. Five years ago we spent 5 percent of our payroll costs on medical insurance. This year we expect this percentage to increase to 15 percent. It is time we do something to reduce these costs. Implementing a wellness center at Carson Corp. can reduce our healthcare costs.

    C. Definition of Terms—For the purpose of this presentation, a wellness center is a program that includes a health club facility, a nutritionist on staff, and classes on health-related issues, such as stress management and smoking cessation.

    D. Plan of Presentation and Scope—Today we will analyze the benefits and costs of implementing a wellness center. We will discuss corporate benefits and costs, as well as employee benefits and costs, followed by a recommendation. At this point, the layout and design of the center will not be discussed. So let's begin by looking at how Carson Corp. can benefit from a wellness center.

The plan of presentation is the last of the five introductory elements. The plan of presentation provides a smooth transition from Building Block #1,

    The Introduction,
    to Building Block #2, The Body.

The Body

The next step in developing the content is to develop Building Block #2, The Body of your presentation. The Body of your presentation develops, organizes, and explains the main ideas you introduced in your presentation introduction.

Developing the Body

The purpose you previously established when organizing your presentation in Phase One will guide you in developing the body of your presentation. All of the information in the Body should support your purpose. Limit the body of your presentation to no more than five main ideas. If you use more than five main ideas in a presentation, it will be difficult for your audience to follow your presentation, and it will be difficult for them to remember all of your ideas.

An effective technique to use when developing the body of your presentation is to outline your main ideas. Then, further develop your outline with supporting data for each main idea.

Developing the Body Example:

1. Introduction (Attention Getter, Background, Scope, Definition of Terms, and Plan of Presentation)

2. Body of Presentation

    a. Corporate Benefits   (MAIN IDEA)
        i.   Decreased healthcare costs
        ii.   Decreased absenteeism   (SUPPORTING
        iii. Decreased stress levels   INFORMATION)
        iv.   Increased productivity

    b. Employee Benefits of Wellness Center   (MAIN IDEA)
        i.   Decreased stress
        ii.   Improved self-image   (SUPPORTING
        iii. Increased socialization   INFORMATION)
        iv.   Decreased healthcare costs

    c. Corporate Costs   (MAIN IDEA)
        i.   . . . .
        ii.   . . . .

    d. Employee Costs   (MAIN IDEA)
        i.   . . . .
        ii.   . . . .

3. Recommendation

Organizing the Body

There are several methods you can use to help you organize the main ideas of the body of your presentation. You can organize by:

- ❑ Chronology
- ❑ Component
- ❑ Importance
- ❑ Cause→Effect→Solution
- ❑ Criteria
- ❑ Topic Pattern

Chronology.   Present the main ideas in the order in which they occurred. This will help your reader to understand the sequential order of development.

Chronology Example:

The history of the development of Quality Circles at XYZ Corp.

How to hire effective employees starting with what should be done first.

Component.   Present the main ideas by division, department, geographical location, etc.

Component Example:

A study on the cost of living in each geographical location.

The planned advertising campaign for each country.

Importance. Present the main ideas in order of importance.

Importance Example:

A presentation on how to organize a conference starting with the most important elements first.

There are seven key steps to take when implementing a telecommuting program.

Cause→Effect→Solution. Present information on the problem, the effect of the problem, and the solution to the problem.

Cause→Effect→Solution Example:

Cause—The organization's high turnover rate.

Effect—Production is down 15 percent.

Solution—Increase salaries and improve the working environment to reduce turnover.

Criteria. To organize by criteria, present information according to the criteria used to evaluate something.

Criteria Example:

Present information on evaluating a new software system using the following criteria: cost, applicability, user friendliness, ease of installation, and compatibility with current software.

Topic Pattern. Divide the topic into logical main ideas, and then organize these ideas in a way that makes sense to you.

Topic Pattern Example:

Present information on a corporate wellness program by discussing the advantages, the disadvantages, and a profile of a current wellness program.

A presentation on conducting business in Brazil may discuss the sociocultural environment, the economic environment, the legal environment, and the business environment.

After planning Building Block #1,

1 The Introduction,
and developing your main ideas with Building Block #2,

1 2 The Body,
it is necessary to connect these ideas using Building Block #3, The Transitional Plan.

1 2 3 *The Transitional Plan*

Using the Transitional Plan

When listening to a presentation, the audience cannot refer back to what the presenter just said, nor can they re-read a section if they do not understand how the main ideas relate to each other. Therefore, it is important for the presenter to guide the audience through the presentation. If the audience cannot logically follow the structure of your presentation, they will lose interest in what you are saying. A presenter provides this guidance by using a Transitional Plan.

The Transitional Plan provides the flow the audience needs to follow your presentation. The Transitional Plan emphasizes the structure of your presentation and leads your audience from one section or idea to the next section or idea. The Transitional Plan provides "signposts" for your audience to tell them where you have been, where you are going, and how your main ideas relate to each other.

There are three parts to the transitional plan:

1. **Lead-In**

2. **Summary**

3. **Transition**

Lead-In

A lead-in introduces each main idea. It reminds the audience where they are in the initial plan of presentation, as well as how the main ideas relate to the overall purpose. The lead-in previews the information that will be discussed in the next part of the presentation.

Below are two examples of lead-ins:

Lead-In Example 1:

The benefits of a corporate wellness center are the first issue that must be analyzed when determining the feasibility of such a center. The benefits are divided into corporate benefits and employee benefits.

(This tells the audience that the presenter will be discussing corporate benefits and employee benefits.)

Lead-In Example 2:

There are three market segments where we are experiencing the most competition: snack foods, diet drinks, and breakfast foods.

(This tells the audience that the presenter will provide information on the three market segments.)

Summary

A summary at the end of each main idea succinctly restates what you have just discussed, repeats how this information relates to the overall purpose, and tells the audience where they are in the context of the presentation.

Below are two examples of summary statements:

Summary Example 1:

As this research shows, our company will benefit from a corporate wellness center because organizations with wellness centers have significantly decreased their healthcare costs, decreased employee absenteeism, and decreased stress levels, resulting in increased productivity.

(These benefits provide a strong incentive for implementing a wellness center.)

Summary Example 2:

In summary, let me review the costs for the wellness center. The initial costs for the building renovation and fitness equipment will be $900,000, and annual operating expenses are estimated at $210,000. Employees will pay $5.00 per month to use the facilities, which will offset the operating costs by $60,000.

After summarizing the information, you need to provide a transition that will guide your audience to the next main idea.

Transition

A transition follows each summary and tells the audience what to expect in the next main idea. Transitions tie the presentation's main ideas or sections together.

Transition Example 1:

The company itself is not the only beneficiary of the wellness program; the employees will also benefit from a wellness center. Let's talk about how employees will benefit.

(This transition tells the audience what the presenter will discuss in the next section of their presentation and how the main ideas relate to each other.)

Transition Example 2:

Now that we understand what virtual reality is, let's look at some examples of how organizations are using virtual reality.

(This transition tells the audience what the presenter will discuss next and how the main ideas relate to each other.)

This three-part transitional plan should be repeated in each section of your presentation. In other words:

1. **Tell them what you are going to tell them** (Lead-in).

2. **Tell them** (Main idea in the body).

3. **Tell them what you just told them** (Summary).

4. **Transition** (Preview what you will discuss next).

The transitions you use should be smooth and logical. Some examples to help you develop transitions are listed on the next page.

a. Now that I have discussed _____ , I would like to tell you about _____.

b. For example, _____.

c. Another topic that we need to consider is _____.

d. The next step in implementing (developing, etc.) is _____ _____.

e. Now that we have looked at the problem, let's talk about some possible solutions, such as _____.

After developing the first three building blocks,

The Introduction,

The Body,
and

The Transitional Plan,
it is time to complete the presentation with Building Block #4, The Conclusion.

The Conclusion

Developing the Conclusion

In your Conclusion section, you will summarize the main ideas and tie together the points you have presented. Emphasize how the main ideas relate to each other and to the presentation's purpose. Remind the audience about the main ideas you presented.

Because your audience is most likely to remember what they hear first and last in a presentation, it is essential that you develop a strong introduction and conclusion.

☞ **Point of Interest**

Depending on your presentation's purpose, your conclusion section should:

❑ Restate your purpose

❑ Summarize your main ideas

❑ Present your conclusions and/or evaluations

❑ Motivate the audience to act, if necessary

❑ Make your recommendation

❑ Provide closure to your presentation

❑ End with a memorable, vivid, positive statement

If you are using the Indirect Plan, your Conclusion section will be the last section of your presentation. If you use the Direct Plan and present your Conclusion section before the Body of your presentation, you need a Closing to your presentation. The Closing tells your audience that you are at the end of your presentation.

The Closing can be short, such as:

> "I would like to answer any questions you may have."

> "That concludes my presentation, thank you for giving me the opportunity to be with you today."

Listed below is the format for each organizational plan.

Indirect	Direct
I. Introduction	I. Introduction
II. Body	II. Conclusion
III. Conclusion	III. Body
IV. Closing	IV. Closing

You have now developed the Introduction, the Body, the Transitional Plan, and the Conclusion sections; however, for your presentation to be complete, it is necessary to also plan for the Question and Answer Session.

Question and Answer Session

The Question and Answer Session is a critical and important part of your presentation. There are different ways to approach the Question and Answer Session. They can be answered during the presentation or postponed until the end of the presentation. As the presenter, you need to determine the most appropriate time to respond to questions.

When deciding when to answer questions, consider that questions asked during your presentation will interrupt the flow; are you comfortable with this arrangement? However, allowing questions during the presentation might provide a more spontaneous, relaxed atmosphere. If you are allotted only so much time, it might be best to hold the questions until after you have finished presenting your introduction, main ideas, and summary.

Once you have decided when to have the Question and Answer Session, be sure to inform your audience of your preference. This can be done in the introduction of your presentation.

To ensure an effective Question and Answer Session, plan for the questions that might be asked before your presentation.

Question and Answer Session Guidelines

The following guidelines will help you prepare for and manage the Question and Answer Session.

1. Anticipate questions when planning your presentation.

2. Encourage questions by:

   • Asking the audience a rhetorical question.

   • Saving interesting statistics or quotes for the question and answer period.

   • Giving participants time to formulate their questions; use silence (a pause for 5–7 seconds) as a catalyst.

   • Positively reinforcing good questions, such as "that's a good question" or "that's a valid point we need to consider."

3. Briefly repeat or reword the question before responding. This makes sure everyone hears the question before it is answered. Repeating the question ensures that you heard the question correctly and also gives you a few seconds to organize your answer.

4. Link questions to the main points made in your presentation. Use the questions as an opportunity to reinforce your presentation's purpose and main ideas.

5. Respond to irrelevant questions by suggesting that the questioner talk with you after the presentation.

(continued)

Question and Answer Session Guidelines *(continued)*

6. Never make up answers; do not be afraid to say "I don't know." Instead, offer to find the answer and report back to the questioner. However, avoid ending your presentation with an I don't know response. Close by stating something you do know.

7. Do not be defensive or aggressive. This is difficult when you are asked a critical or attacking question. Take a deep breath, remain calm, and respond to any parts of the question you can.

   - You may even want to comment on the questioner's perspective or insight to help diffuse the hostility. If you cannot satisfy this person, offer to talk with him/her after the presentation.

   - Remember, if you remain calm, chances are your audience will empathize with you and not with the attacking questioner.

8. Know when to bring the question and answer session to a close. When the questions subside or your audience is getting off the subject, bring the question and answer session to a formal close. For example:

   - "If there are no other questions . . ."

   - "We have covered all of the information and answered questions concerning ABC Company's Corporate Wellness Center. At our next meeting we will . . ."

Phase Two: Developing the Content Summary

There are four building blocks to use when Developing the Content of your presentation. By systematically developing the content of each building block—the Introduction, the Body, the Transitional Plan, and the Conclusion—you will have prepared a presentation that meets your audience's needs, is interesting, and is easy for your audience to understand.

Use the Planning Guides on pages 49–54 to develop your presentation outline. Additional planning guides may be found in the appendix. The Developing the Content Checklist on page 55 will guide you when developing your content.

Now that you have planned and developed the content of the presentation, you can move on to Phase Three: Creating and Using Visual Aids.

The Introduction

The Body

The Transitional Plan

The Conclusion

Phase Two: Introduction Planning Guide

Presentation Purpose _____

_____

I. Introduction

Attention Getter _____

_____

_____

_____

Background _____

_____

_____

_____

Scope _____

_____

_____

_____

Terms to Define _____

_____

_____

Plan of Presentation _____

_____

_____

_____

Phase Two: Developing the Body Planning Guide

Purpose _____

_____

First Main Idea _____

    Lead-in _____

    Support _____

_____

    Support _____

_____

    Support _____

_____

    Support _____

_____

    Summary _____

_____

    Transition _____

_____

(continued)

Phase Two: Developing the Body
Planning Guide *(continued)*

Second Main Idea _____

    Lead-in _____

    Support _____

    _____

    Support _____

    _____

    Support _____

    _____

    Support _____

    _____

    Summary _____

    _____

    Transition _____

    _____

(continued)

Phase Two: Developing the Body Planning Guide *(continued)*

Third Main Idea _____

    Lead-in _____

    Support _____

    _____

    Support _____

    _____

    Support _____

    _____

    Support _____

    _____

    Summary _____

    _____

    Transition _____

    _____

(continued)

Phase Two: Developing the Body
Planning Guide *(continued)*

Fourth Main Idea _____

    Lead-in _____

    Support _____

    _____

    Support _____

    _____

    Support _____

    _____

    Support _____

    _____

    Summary _____

    _____

    _____

    _____

Phase Two: Developing the Conclusion Planning Guide

Purpose _____

_____

_____

Summarize Main Ideas

1. _____

2. _____

3. _____

4. _____

5. _____

Recommendation / Evaluation / Conclusion

_____

_____

_____

_____

_____

_____

_____

_____

_____

_____

_____

Phase Two: Developing the Content Checklist

Introduction

❑ Does your introduction include all of the following elements?
- ❑ Attention Getter
- ❑ Background
- ❑ Scope
- ❑ Definition of Terms (if needed)
- ❑ Plan of Presentation

❑ Does your introduction motivate the audience to listen and establish your credibility?

❑ Do you tell your audience why your presentation is important and what they will learn from the presentation?

Body

❑ Are you presenting three to five main ideas?

❑ Are your ideas presented in a logical order?

❑ Do you use the transitional plan?

❑ Does every main idea include a lead-in, summary, and transition?

Conclusion

❑ Do you summarize your main ideas?

❑ Have you clearly stated your recommendation/evaluation/conclusion?

❑ Are you ending with a vivid positive statement?

Questions and Answers

❑ Have you decided when to hold the question and answer session?

❑ Have you thought about what questions the audience might ask?

Phase Two: Presentation Challenge

Choose a topic (implementing a telecommuting program, developing an e-commerce business, recommending a new sales strategy, etc.) and complete this worksheet.

Identify the purpose of the presentation. _____

_____

_____

_____

_____

Identify the three to five main ideas.

1. _____

   _____

2. _____

   _____

3. _____

   _____

4. _____

   _____

5. _____

   _____

(continued)

Phase Two: Presentation Challenge
(*continued*)

List the supporting points for each main idea.

1. _____
   _____

2. _____
   _____

3. _____
   _____

4. _____
   _____

5. _____
   _____

Develop the conclusion by summarizing/recommending.

_____

_____

_____

Develop the introduction by writing the attention getter, background information, scope, and plan of presentation.

_____

_____

_____

_____

PHASE THREE:
CREATING AND
USING VISUAL AIDS

The third phase, **Creating and Using Visual Aids** is a critical component of effective presentations.

This phase includes four building blocks.

⬚1 ***Selecting the Appropriate Medium***

⬚1⬚2 ***Creating the Design***

⬚1⬚2⬚3 ***Choosing the Appropriate Diagram***

⬚1⬚2⬚3⬚4 ***Presenting the Visuals***

Visual aids can enhance the presenter's image, replace the presenter's notes, improve the audience's comprehension, and increase the audience's retention rate.

☞ **Point of Interest**

It has been said that people generally remember:

❑ 20 percent of what they hear

❑ 30 percent of what they see

❑ 50 to 85 percent of what they hear and see

Therefore, as a presenter you should not rely solely on the audience's sense of hearing to understand your message. Appeal to as many different senses as appropriate when presenting to assist your audience in retaining information. It is important to use more than just words when presenting. Words are verbal symbols with attached interpretations—sometimes multiple interpretations.

By using a variety of delivery techniques you will not only increase retention rates, but you will also accommodate the diverse learning styles of the individuals in your audience. In addition, studies have revealed that the use of well-prepared visuals have been known to motivate an audience to act.

Two types of visual aids can be used to enhance the verbal part of your presentation—text and graphic. Text visuals consist of words that are used to outline and summarize your presentation. Graphics are visuals used to illustrate key concepts or numerical data.

☞ **Point of Interest**

To enhance your presentation, visual aids should:

❑ Relate to your presentation's purpose,

❑ Demonstrate one key concept per visual,

❑ Be relevant, honest, and accurate,

❑ Be simple, clear, consistent, and easy to read,

❑ Use contrast and color to emphasize key points,

❑ Minimize text, emphasize pictures and graphics, and

❑ Be large enough to be read in the back of the room.

When developing the content of your presentation, consider the concepts that need to be emphasized. You can then represent these concepts both verbally and visually. The four building blocks of the third phase of building an effective presentation, Creating and Using Visuals Aids, will assist you in incorporating visual aids effectively into your presentation.

1️⃣ *Selecting the Appropriate Medium*

The medium you select to emphasize your presentation content depends on the purpose of your presentation, the audience analysis, and the technology you feel most comfortable using. The media available today ranges on a continuum from simple to sophisticated.

Let's start with the simple.

Handouts

Using handouts is an easy and inexpensive
way to create visuals.

Visuals can be distributed as handouts
when you want to provide the audience
with an agenda of the presentation, when
you have a great deal of information to
share, when the information being
delivered would be difficult to display using
another medium, when you want to provide the audience an outline
for taking notes, or when you want to provide the audience
information for future use.

A common question asked is, "When should the handouts be
distributed?" If the audience needs to use the handouts throughout the
presentation, then by all means distribute them before the presentation
starts. For example, if you prepare a copy of the presentation agenda or
an outline for notetaking, place these handouts on the desks or tables
prior to the audience arriving. However, if the handouts pertain to one
section of your presentation, distribute them at the appropriate time.
Understand that interrupting the flow of the presentation to distribute
handouts might create a distraction.

It is important to remember that handouts can be a distracter for both
you and the audience. If the audience has access to handouts during
the presentation, you might have to compete for the audience's
attention. Ask yourself, if you lose the audience's attention, will you
ever get it back? Another option is to distribute the handouts after your
presentation. If this is your desire, make an announcement of your
intent during the introduction of the presentation.

Props

If a verbal description or a picture does not adequately enhance your concept, consider using a prop. For example, when discussing an ergonomic keyboard, a picture of the keyboard would not tell the true story. The best visual would be the actual keyboard. When using props, remember to hold or demonstrate it so that everyone can see. Or, position it on a stand that everyone has access  to. Avoid passing props through the audience—this is distracting. The use of props works best with small audiences.

Flipcharts

Flipcharts are one of the most popular and economical media to use when making presentations. The pages on a flipchart can be prepared ahead of time or you can use them spontaneously. Position the easel so that everyone can see. Obviously, this medium does not work well when presenting to a large audience. The audience size, when using a flipchart, should not exceed 40–50 people.

Point of Interest

When preparing a flipchart, consider the following guidelines:

- ❑ Print the text or graphic on the top two-thirds of the page,
- ❑ Print each letter at least two to three inches tall,
- ❑ Use bold letters,
- ❑ Leave white space,
- ❑ Leave a blank page after each printed page, and
- ❑ Use color, but don't overdo.

When preparing the flipchart, leave a blank page between printed pages so that the prepared text or graphic will not show through and so that the visual is removed when you turn the page. Furthermore, blank pages will allow you to make additional notes during your presentation, if necessary, without having to turn through the series of prepared visuals to find a blank page. At times the page turning can be cumbersome, especially when searching for a certain visual to review a second time. When preparing the flipchart, consider the pages that the audience might want to review and attach a plastic tab for easy reference. The plastic tabs will also help you when turning the pages.

Flipcharts allow the presenter to pencil in reminders. Take advantage of this tip—the audience will not see your notes. Use flipcharts to enhance an informal presentation environment. Consider using them when the presentation is interactive. You can spread several charts around the perimeter of the room so the audience can use them as well.

Flipcharts are inexpensive, relatively easy to create, and available in most presentation environments.

Boards

The traditional black board has been replaced with white boards in most presentation environments. However, the major downfall is true of both—what goes on, must come off. When writing and erasing, you interrupt the flow of the presentation, and eye contact with audience is broken. Limit

the use of boards to impromptu writing or drawing and only when the presentation environment is informal.

Overhead Projectors

Overhead projectors provide an easy and inexpensive means of projecting visuals. Transparencies can be created ahead of time or can be created with marking pens during the presentation. By using computer presentation software programs, a variety of sophisticated slides can be created within a short period of time.

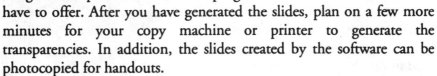

Take advantage of the professionally designed templates the software programs have to offer. After you have generated the slides, plan on a few more minutes for your copy machine or printer to generate the transparencies. In addition, the slides created by the software can be photocopied for handouts.

Most presentation environments maintain projectors; so if you are traveling, the transparencies are no burden. In addition, the transparencies are easy to store and update. Even though there are many reasons to use this medium, there is one downfall—they are only effective when presenting to small or medium-sized audiences.

Slides, 35 mm

The image a slide show projects can be impressive, and the cost of preparing and developing slides has decreased. Slides are easy to transport, effective when displaying photographs, and appropriate for larger audiences. Many of today's software programs will allow you to generate the slides on your own computer. When preparing for your presentation, plan on inserting a blank slide between slides so that a blank screen appears when you are talking. Or turn the machine off.

There are several major drawbacks when presenting with slides. The lights must be dimmed, which draws the audience's attention away from the presenter and directs it to the slides only. Also, the order of the slide presentation is difficult to change once the slides have been arranged in the carousel. In addition, slides are difficult to alter once they have been created.

Videos

More and more business presenters are using videos or video clips. This medium is popular because videos are entertaining and most meeting rooms are equipped with the necessary technology. In addition, the price of creating a video is going down daily, and the videos available for rental are unlimited.

Videos are appropriate for demonstrations; however, when using them, the focus is shifted from the presenter to the video. Some experts suggest showing no more than a 30-second video. If using a video for an extended period of time, consider showing one clip at a time. For example, if you are using the video for a demonstration or training, show clips and reserve the time between clips for discussion and audience interaction. Plan ahead by preparing questions for discussion so that the video is not the sole source of contribution.

Computer Presentations

Computer generated slide shows are a common presentation medium. The main advantage of this medium is the ease and timeliness with which you can create and alter your presentation. The output, whether it be slides or the image on the computer screen, can be projected by an overhead projector or a projection system. As with some of the options already discussed, this medium can require dimming the lights for a clear projection.

☞ Point of Interest

PowerPoint Tips:

❏ Think about how you can use graphics to communicate your text. One of the most powerful tools available to you for telling your story is the effective use of graphics.

❏ Place graphics in the lower, right-hand corner of your slide.

❏ Stick with one or two non-distracting slide transitions.

❏ Use sound effects sparingly and make sure they add appropriate impact.

❏ Use a different color slide for the beginning of each major section of your presentation. This lets the audience know you are transitioning to a new topic.

❏ Use font size to show the hierarchy of your ideas. For example, the title of the slide should be larger than the font size of the bulleted points:

Title—28–42 pts.

Text—24–28 pts.

❏ Choose an interesting and appropriate font. For example, some fonts present a more formal image than others.

❏ Use no more than three different fonts in a presentation.

❏ Use slide titles that engage the audience's attention.

❏ Learn to show the presentation—practice using the equipment.

❏ Project the presentation in the room where you will present ahead of time so you can adjust the color scheme and font sizes, if needed.

❏ Manually run your actual presentation instead of using the automated feature. Your timing may change during your presentation due to a faster or slower speaking rate. With the automated feature you cannot adapt your presentation to answer questions or further explain a certain topic.

Multimedia

The latest technology to appear in business presentations is the combined efforts of text, graphics, video, and audio—otherwise known as multimedia. A multimedia presentation, obviously, can be very impressive. An overwhelming amount of information can be customized for a particular audience.

Depending on the audience, you can include or omit parts of the presentation. At the same time, you can advance and return as you see fit.

The technology necessary to create multimedia presentations calls for an up-to-date computer with the appropriate capabilities. In addition, the presentation room must be outfitted with both sound and image projection equipment, and preferably a wireless mouse.

As with all presentation media, the razzle and dazzle one can create does not replace a sound, well-prepared presentation. The combination of relevant visuals and the effective creation of the visuals is essential for success. After you have finished

> **Selecting the Appropriate Medium,**
> the following guidelines will help you with Building Block #2, Creating the Design.

1 2 *Creating the Design*

Your audience has a brief period to study and comprehend your visuals, so they should be well designed and sparingly used. Resist the temptation to go into "visual aid overload." Remember to Create the Design of the visual with the audience and presentation environment in mind. The following design guidelines will help you.

Color

Color attracts attention and increases your audience's willingness to pay attention to your visuals. Color will enable you to emphasize key points, differentiate sections, add authenticity, and improve the presentation image.

☞ Point of Interest

When using color, consider the following guidelines:

- ❑ Use color sparingly and with purpose. The benefits of color can be lost if too many are used.

- ❑ Use consistent colors for backgrounds, logos, and similar elements. Common colors indicate a relationship or similarity.

- ❑ Use brightness or immerse an area in color to attract the audience's attention.

- ❑ Link the magnitude of the color change with the event change.

- ❑ Use realistic colors—grass should be green.

❑ Reds, oranges, and yellows are warm colors and should be used to indicate strength, energy, and action.

❑ Violets, blues, and greens, are cool colors and are appropriate for background colors because they generate feelings of relaxation and passiveness.

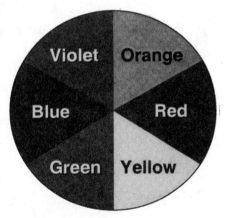

❑ Conservative colors (blue) add formality and brighter colors (orange) create a more informal and somewhat trendy look.

❑ There are many ways to use color. If you desire harmony, choose a combination of either warm colors or cool colors. If you desire complementary colors, choose colors opposite each other on the color wheel—red and green, orange and blue, or yellow and violet. Many software programs have preset color combinations that you can choose for the background, title, and text or graphics. Choose this option if you want the program to determine the color selections.

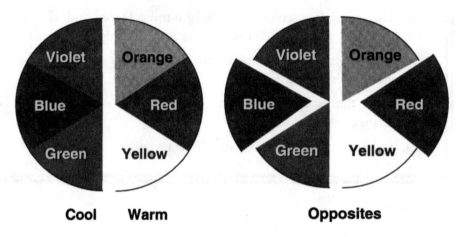

Cool   Warm   Opposites

❑ Be consistent in your use of color throughout your presentation. Your audience will then be able to associate color with the intended meaning. Do not make your audience work to understand the relationship.

❑ Remember, the color you see on your computer monitor might differ from the color projected in your presentation environment.

Format

Format, used correctly, will help you deliver your message. Format concerns the shape and size of your visual. Audience members tend to look at the upper, left-hand corner first—use this area for important information. Eyes tend to move from left to right—use this pattern to indicate a flow. The next direction eyes generally move is from top to bottom.

Horizontal lines indicate stability, vertical lines indicate growth or action, and broken or jagged lines indicate inconsistency. When including a logo on your visuals, place it so that it is not the most prominent element.

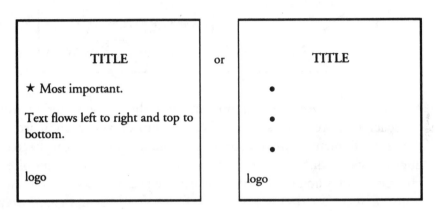

Balance

Balance is the arrangement of elements on your visual. Use a vertical format for the text with bullets or graphics separating lines of text. Follow the 6 × 7 rule, which limits the lines of text to six and the words per line to seven. On text visuals use both upper- and lowercase letters.

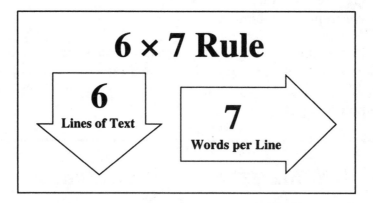

The spacing between the heading and text should be different from the spacing between lines of text. Leave a considerable margin around the text. (Remember that your visual, when projected on a screen, might appear different than that on your computer monitor.) However, too much blank space diverts the audience's attention away from the text. Use decorative bars to frame your visual; be consistent when choosing the bars and the color.

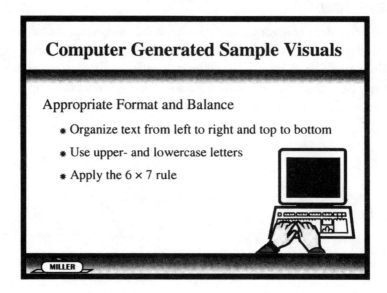

Readability

Readability is often overlooked when creating visuals. Everyone in the room must be able to see and read your visuals with ease. Use solid letters and fonts of no less than 24 points in size for computer-generated visuals.

24-point font size

When formatting your visuals, remember to consider the color, format, balance, and readability to create your visuals effectively.

You have spent time

1   **Selecting the Appropriate Medium** and

1 2   **Creating the Design.**
It is also necessary to consider Building Block #3, Choosing the Appropriate Diagram.

1 2 3   *Choosing the Appropriate Diagram*

The appropriate diagram will help you convey your message. Consider the following options.

Bar Graphs

Bar graphs should be used to compare sizes of several items, show changes over time, and show the components of a whole and the relative sizes. The bars can be vertical or horizontal, solid or shaded, or made up of pictures, such as cars. Remember, each bar should be labeled with the size, total, or dollar amount depicting the bar.

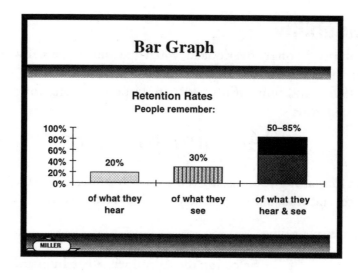

Flow Charts

Flow charts should be used to show a series of steps from the beginning to the end and to show relationships.

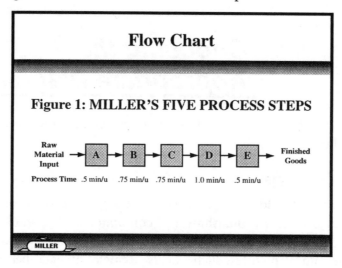

Line Graphs

Line graphs should be used to indicate changes over time of one or more variables. Remember to label the peaks and valleys on the lines with a word description or a number.

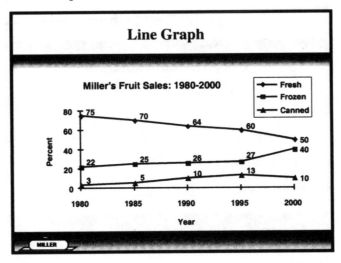

Maps

Maps should be used to represent geographic areas or locational relationships.

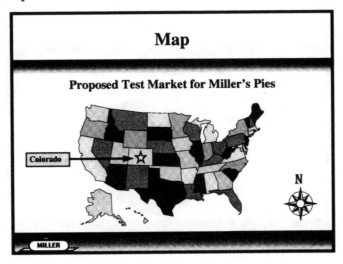

Organizational Charts

Organizational charts should be used to show the interrelationships within an organization.

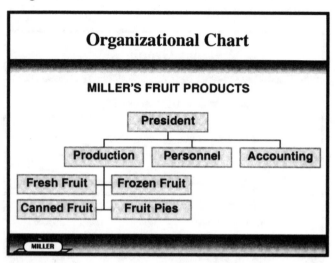

Pie Charts

Pie charts should be used to show the pieces of a whole and their relative sizes. Remember, the pieces of the pie should total 100 percent.

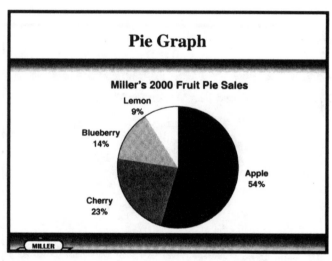

Tables

Tables are used to present detailed, technical information and survey results. Highlight the primary element you want to emphasize.

Table

Miller's 2000 Fruit Pie Sales				
Fruit Flavor	Apple	Cherry	Blueberry	Lemon
Total	5400	2300	1400	900
Percentage	54	23	14	9

MILLER

Selecting the Appropriate Medium, Creating the Design, and Choosing the Appropriate Diagram will all contribute to the generation of effective visuals. In addition, a few general guidelines will help you when planning and preparing your visual aids. A practical rule of thumb to follow is to avoid more than five different mechanics on any one visual. Mechanics consist of colors, fonts, type styles, bold print, underlines, and graphics. A combination of more than five of the above creates an overwhelmingly busy visual.

When developing effective visuals, the key building blocks are

1   Selecting the Appropriate Medium,

1 2   Creating the Design,
and

1 2 3   Choosing the Appropriate Diagram.
To utilize your visuals effectively, it is necessary to add Building Block #4, Presenting the Visuals.

1 2 3 4 *Presenting the Visuals*

The next step when using visuals is to concentrate on incorporating them smoothly into your presentation. In other words, practice makes perfect.

When using visual aids, start by introducing the visual before explaining it. Do not read the visual to the audience; instead, concentrate on summarizing important points.

Continue to establish rapport with the audience by maintaining eye contact when explaining the visual aid. Talk to your audience, not to the visual aid. However, initially, you can direct a glance or two towards the visual so that the audience will relate your discussion to the visual aid.

It is imperative that you allow the audience time to comprehend the information. Remember that the information you are conveying is new to the audience—it will take them longer to digest the concept. Provide the audience at least 20 seconds to view the visual after you have introduced it and before you discuss it.

Point of Interest

The following tips will help you incorporate your visuals smoothly into your presentation.

- ❑ Consistently prepare the visuals.
- ❑ Number overheads and handouts.
- ❑ Clearly and concisely word the visual headings.
- ❑ Stand facing the audience.
- ❑ Stand next to the flipchart or projector screen but never between your visual and the audience.
- ❑ Point with the hand closest to the visual.
- ❑ Remove the visual when you are finished.

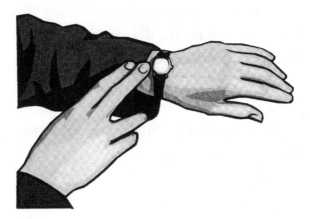

Essential to any business presentation is the final once over prior to the presentation. **Arrive at least 30 minutes early** to allow yourself plenty of time for a thorough check. Use the checklist on page 82 when reviewing your presentation environment.

Phase Three: Presentation Environment Checklist

Before presenting, check the following:

- ❏ Is the furniture arranged so that everyone can see you and your visuals?
- ❏ Are the power outlets functioning?
  - ❏ Do you need an extension cord?
  - ❏ Will the cord be in your way?
- ❏ Is the necessary equipment functioning properly?
- ❏ Is the lighting correctly adjusted and can you access the controls?
- ❏ Is there a table on which to rest your visuals?
- ❏ Do you have extra copies of your handouts?
- ❏ Do you have your emergency presentation kit?
  - ❏ Extra copy of computer disk containing visuals
  - ❏ Transparencies in case of computer failure
  - ❏ Extension cord
  - ❏ Extra projector bulb
  - ❏ Extra markers for flipcharts, transparencies, etc.
  - ❏ Blank transparencies
  - ❏ Cup for water
  - ❏ Throat lozenges
  - ❏ Business cards

Phase Three: Creating and Using Visual Aids Summary

Building Blocks 1–4, Selecting the Appropriate Medium, Creating the Design, Choosing the Appropriate Diagram, and Presenting the Visuals, should be used to structure Phase Three. However, even the most impressive visuals cannot camouflage a poorly planned presentation. Visual aids should be used to supplement the presentation, not dominate it; remember that some concepts need explanation more than others. Use visuals to ensure that each audience member receives a uniform message. And do not forget, PROOFREAD your visuals while you still have time to make corrections.

Use the Visual Aid Checklist on page 84 to help you utilize visual aids effectively.

1   *Selecting the Appropriate Medium*

1 2   *Creating the Design*

1 2 3   *Choosing the Appropriate Diagram*

1 2 3 4   *Presenting the Visuals*

Phase Three: Visual Aid Checklist

After you have viewed your presentation practice session on videotape, ask yourself these questions about visual aids.

- ❑ Do the visuals dominate the presentation?
- ❑ Do the visuals illustrate how and why?
- ❑ Does each visual emphasize important information?
- ❑ Does each visual emphasize only one concept?
- ❑ Are the visuals prepared consistently?
- ❑ Are the headings descriptive but concise?
- ❑ Is the lettering bold and large enough?
- ❑ Has color been used effectively?
- ❑ Was color used to emphasize key concepts?
- ❑ Have similar colors been used to emphasize similar items?
- ❑ Are the color changes linked to the changes or degrees of meaning?
- ❑ Are the background colors and/or designs distracting?
- ❑ Was the most appropriate medium chosen?
- ❑ Was the design linked to the concept being conveyed?
- ❑ Was the audience's view blocked?
- ❑ Was the visual easy to see at the back of the room?
- ❑ Was the closest hand used to point to the visual?
- ❑ Was the 6 × 7 rule applied?
- ❑ Was the visual removed when not in use?
- ❑ Was the equipment turned off when not in use?
- ❑ Do the visual aids improve the presentation?

Phase Three: Presentation Challenge

Indicate what the best visual aid would be for the following circumstances:

1. Presenting detailed results about the quality improvement records for each department.

    _____

2. Compare the sales for each division in the company for each quarter of the year.

    _____

3. Show the President's approval ratings during the four years he was in office.

    _____

4. Present the workflow to manufacture a mountain bike.

    _____

5. Show each division's contribution to the company's profit.

    _____

PHASE FOUR:
DELIVERING THE PRESENTATION

Phase Four, **Delivering the Presentation** is the final phase in an effective presentation. Effective presenters are made, not born; effectively delivering a presentation is a skill you can learn. And the best way to learn a skill is to practice. As the old saying goes, "practice makes perfect."

Excellent speaking is the combination of doing many things well. The steps you have already completed in the first three phases will contribute to the success of your presentation. In addition, mastering effective delivery techniques will make you an effective presenter.

Your goal is to deliver a presentation so your audience understands, accepts, and remembers what you say. This will involve mastering the skills discussed in Phase Four's three building blocks:

1 *Verbal Skills*

1 2 *Non-verbal Skills*

1 2 3 *Presentation Style*

☐ *Verbal Skills*

Word Usage

Use conversational language, words that everyone in your audience will understand. Follow these guidelines when selecting the words for your presentation.

❑ **Use active voice.** When using active voice, the subject performs the action. For example:

❑ "We can save you money" versus "Money can be saved by us."

❑ **Use personal language and pronouns.** For example:

❑ "Our problem" versus "The problem."

❑ **Use short words and short sentences.** For example:

Long	Short
ascertain	learn
circumvent	avoid
peruse	read

When people talk to each other, short and simple words are used; practice this same pattern when delivering a presentation. The presentation will be easier to comprehend and sound more natural. Dictionaries are not available during your presentation—therefore do not use unfamiliar words.

❑ **Paint word pictures to help the audience visualize and retain your message.** Your goal is for your audience to have the same image in their mind as you have in yours. Be specific in your descriptions or use an analogy to illustrate your point. For example:

Unspecific: The quality circle program was effective.

Specific: The quality circle program generated 10 ideas that saved the company $1,000,000.

Unspecific: These brakes stop a car within a short distance.

Specific: These XYZ anti-lock brakes stop a 2-ton car, traveling 60 miles an hour, within 240 feet.

Analogy: Merging the two departments was like trying to mix oil and water.

❑ **Eliminate non-words and filler phrases.** A careless choice of words may cause listeners to tune you out, resulting in a bored or turned off audience. For example:

Non-words: "uh, uhmm, y' know"

Filler phrases: "you know what I mean," "kind of," "and like um."

Vocals

When making a presentation, you want your audience to understand and remember the content. To do this, make it easy for them to hear what you say. The vocal part of your presentation involves:

- ❑ Pronunciation
- ❑ Vocal inflections
- ❑ Tone
- ❑ Rate
- ❑ Volume

Pronunciation.   Use only words that you can comfortably pronounce. Make sure you practice the correct pronunciation of the words you plan on using. Pronouncing words incorrectly will decrease your credibility and make you sound unprepared.

Vocal Inflections. Your vocal inflection or pitch should be varied and natural. Talking in a monotone voice is one of the biggest problems for presenters. Avoid using the same pitch throughout your presentation as the monotony of this will quickly bore your audience.

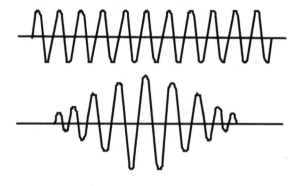

Point of Interest

- ❑ Generally, the lower the pitch the more calm and confident you will sound.

- ❑ Nervousness contracts and tightens the muscles around the throat and voice box. This may cause the pitch you use to rise when you present.

- ❑ Practice into a tape recorder so can hear how you sound and adjust your vocals accordingly.

Tone. Remember it is not only what you say but how you say it that conveys meaning to your audience. Your tone should be objective and neutral. If the tone of your voice becomes condescending or preachy or if it conveys an "attitude," you may lose your credibility.

A speaker's tones naturally tend to rise at the end of a question and fall at the end of a statement. Even though it is difficult to hear your own tone accurately, you can probably listen to how your tone changes as you say each sentence when you are practicing your presentation. Recording your presentation when you practice is the best way to evaluate your tone.

Rate. Good presenters vary their pace and use pauses effectively. A good "rule of thumb" is to talk quickly for a while, slow down at a key point, and then pause. It is a good idea to be deliberate at times to emphasize important points.

The average speaking rate is 125 words per minute; however, the average person can process 400 words per minute. Therefore, the mind has time to wander if the speaker's rate is too slow.

The key is to vary your speaking rate to hold your audience's attention. You will need to practice your presentation to determine when to speak rapidly, when to pause, and when to speak slowly to emphasize key ideas.

Volume.   Project your voice so that the audience members in the back row of the room can hear you. But remember, you also need to vary the volume or loudness of your voice. You can speak louder to draw attention to a key point or you can speak softer. Even a whisper can be used to vary your volume and to keep your audience's attention.

Also, consider any distracting noises that might interfere with being heard and adjust your volume accordingly. You will need to speak louder when presenting to an audience than you would when practicing in an empty room.

Remember to:

- ❑ **Speak out**
- ❑ **Speak clearly**
- ❑ **Speak to be understood**

Practicing your vocals will ensure that your presentation is varied but sounds natural and comfortable. A good way to practice your presentation is to use a tape recorder so you can listen to your vocals as your audience would hear them.

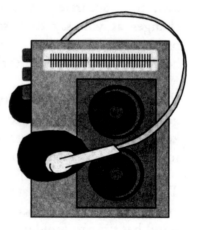

"It is not sufficient to know what one ought to say; one must also know how to say it."

— Aristotle

Building Block #1,

| 1 | Verbal Skills,
contribute to a successful presentation. In addition, your success also depends upon the non-verbal aspect of communicating. These skills are addressed in Building Block #2, Non-verbal Skills.

1 2 Non-verbal Skills

Studies show that 60–90 percent of a presentation's overall effect comes from non-verbal cues. Therefore, it is important to develop positive non-verbal skills to support and enhance your verbal skills. The important point to remember is that your non-verbal message should support and agree with the verbal message you are delivering. If your non-verbal and verbal message conflict, your audience will believe and remember your non-verbals instead of your words.

Your audience's impression begins to form when you come into view and continues to develop until you are out of sight. Your non-verbals will either enhance your credibility and believability with your audience or they will undermine your message.

For example, if at the beginning of your presentation you tell your audience how happy you are to be there but you are frowning and looking at your watch, the audience will not believe your words because your body language is contradicting what you are saying.

The non-verbal aspect of your presentation includes posture and movement, gestures, eye contact and smile, all of which contribute to your overall image.

Posture and Movement

Your posture should be dignified but relaxed. A reliable rule of thumb is to stand up straight, throw your shoulders back, and breathe from your diaphragm. Do not be rigid, but look your best and at the same time look comfortable and confident.

A dignified but relaxed posture can add immeasurably to the delivery of your message. When the speaker is comfortable and relaxed, the audience will be too.

Posture can also be used to dictate the formality or informality of your presentation. A formal presenter stands behind the podium. An informal presenter stands next to the podium and moves around the room. The building blocks of Phase One, Defining the Presentation's Purpose and Analyzing the Audience, will help you determine the degree of formality that is most appropriate for each presentation.

Effective presenters find a balance between standing stiffly behind a podium and moving too much across the front of the room. Even during formal presentations it is beneficial to move from the podium into the audience at some point during the presentation.

Point of Interest

Guidelines for Effective Posture and Movement

❑ Stand up straight, feet slightly apart, arms comfortable and ready to gesture.

❑ Avoid keeping a "white knuckle" grip on the podium or lectern. This does not convey confidence.

❑ Avoid swaying back and forth or pacing too much across the front of the room.

❑ Avoid standing with your arms folded across your chest; this displays the classic "I'm defensive" posture.

❑ Avoid standing with your arms hanging straight at your sides for the entire presentation or with your arms behind your back. You will look unnatural and uncomfortable.

❑ Avoid leaving your hands inside your pockets for the entire presentation. Occasionally putting one hand in your pocket is acceptable.

❑ Avoid speaking with your head bowed. Look out at the audience and establish eye contact.

This list may seem full of "don'ts" regarding posture. These "don'ts" emphasize the need to practice your presentation so you can develop posture and movements that you are comfortable with and that convey credibility and confidence. The best way to assess your posture and movements is to videotape your practice session.

Effective use of posture helps to create a positive non-verbal impression conveying confidence. The gestures you use will also help you to effectively communicate your message.

Gestures

Use gestures to enhance your words and for effect. Gestures are important when making both formal and informal presentations.

Vary your gestures so they are natural and meaningful. It is better not to plan your gestures, but to plan the ideas you want to stress, and naturally use gestures at these times. The following guidelines will aid you in effectively using gestures.

☞ **Point of Interest**

Guidelines for Effectively Using Gestures

❑ Make sure your gestures can be seen over the podium and from the back of the room.

❑ Plan on using gestures to emphasize ideas and to enhance points about size, number, and direction.

❑ Practice what to do with your hands when not gesturing. Rest your hands lightly at your sides or on a table or lectern between gestures.

Be sure to avoid distracting gestures, ones that presenters use because they are nervous or distracted. The presenter is rarely aware of using distracting gestures, but the audience will be painfully aware of them.

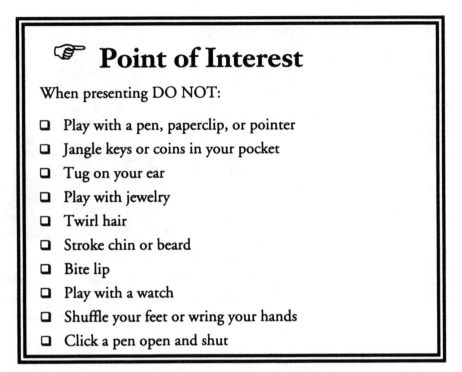

☞ **Point of Interest**

When presenting DO NOT:

- ❑ Play with a pen, paperclip, or pointer
- ❑ Jangle keys or coins in your pocket
- ❑ Tug on your ear
- ❑ Play with jewelry
- ❑ Twirl hair
- ❑ Stroke chin or beard
- ❑ Bite lip
- ❑ Play with a watch
- ❑ Shuffle your feet or wring your hands
- ❑ Click a pen open and shut

These distracting gestures will cause your audience to pay attention to the distracting gesture and not to your content. Practicing your presentation in front of a video camera will show you what distracting gestures (if any) you have a tendency to use. Once you are aware of any distracting gestures, you can work to eliminate them from your presentation.

Effectively using gestures will enhance the words you speak, convey that you are relaxed and comfortable, and have a positive impact on the audience. In addition to effectively using gestures, it is necessary to make a conscious decision to use eye contact and smile to complete the effectiveness of your non-verbal skills.

Eye Contact and Smile

Eye contact establishes rapport with your audience and lends credibility to your presentation. It can bridge the gap between you and your audience. Making eye contact will give the audience the feeling that they are being individually addressed instead of being addressed as an anonymous mass.

Eye contact encourages effective listening. To establish eye contact, find a friendly face and address a sentence or two to him or her. Maintain eye contact with this individual for three to six seconds, working the room so that everyone feels included. Do not look at one spot in the back of the room, use darting glances, or form an eye contact pattern—side, back, side.

Eye contact can be used to encourage audience participation if your presentation's purpose calls for interaction. Eye contact with the audience also gives you feedback on how you are doing—is the audience interested, do they understand what you are saying, do they agree with you, and are they relating to your ideas. Your audience is communicating with you non-verbally during your entire presentation and you should use this feedback to your advantage. Another non-verbal skill you can use to your advantage is a smile.

Smile and people will smile back. A sincere smile puts your audience as well as yourself at ease and encourages positive feelings.

It is a myth that business presenters must be stonefaced, stuffy, and boring. An expressionless face is not a prerequisite to being an effective, credible presenter; in fact, it could deter from the effectiveness of your presentation. Learn to relax and let your personality come through. Business presentations can be effective and at the same time enjoyable. If you are smiling and comfortable, the audience will react the same way.

An effective delivery involves

1 Verbal Skills,
which will help you deliver an understandable and memorable presentation, and

1 2 Non-verbal Skills,
which include posture and movement, gestures, and eye contact and smile. Non-verbal forms of communication will have an incredible impact on the success of your presentation.

Building Block #3, Presentation Style, is also a key contributor to an effective presentation.

1 2 3 *Presentation Style*

Style is the undefinable element that can make you a powerful and effective presenter. In addition to providing excellent content that is well delivered, style is what makes people want to clap at the end of your presentation, is what makes people remember you the next day, makes your audience feel good, makes your audience want to ask you back, and is what makes people in the audience want to emulate you when they make a presentation.

There is no one perfect presentation style. There are many excellent presenters who have very different presentation styles.

The most important thing to remember about style is that you have to develop your own. Your presentation will fail if you try to be someone you are not. If you "act," the audience will see through the charade. So, how do you develop your own style?

Style is developed over time and is based on your unique personality. Style is a mixture of enthusiasm, intelligence, confidence, charisma, preparation, originality, and sincerity. Style is the overall excellence and grace of a good presenter.

To enhance your style include and appropriately use

❑   Greetings and closings,

❑   Humor, and

❑   Notes.

Greetings and Closings

Audience members typically remember what they hear first and what they hear last. Therefore, take advantage of these key opportunities to provide a strong opening and closing. A positive first impression, conveying credibility, self-confidence, warmth, and friendliness sets the stage for the presentation. Walk to the podium, pause, make eye contact for three to five seconds, then sincerely smile and greet your audience. By doing this, you will give both a verbal and non-verbal hello. A sincere greeting will convey that you are interested in your audience and that you are pleased to be presenting to them.

It is a good idea to have a well-planned greeting because some presenters tend to be more nervous during the first two to three minutes of the presentation. So, spend some extra time planning the first few minutes of your introduction. This will increase your confidence and ensure an effective greeting.

Also, spend time planning a memorable close. During the close, repeat your main idea, offer a quote or challenge, provide a link to your attention getter, or end with a clear statement of action desired. Avoid closing with an empty statement like "thanks for coming, I guess that's all I have to say."

Just as you gave your audience a verbal and non-verbal "hello," you should also give a verbal and non-verbal goodbye. Be sure that you do not walk away from the front of the room or the podium until you have given your audience a verbal goodbye, a smile, and a non-verbal goodbye.

By following all of the guidelines discussed in Developing an Introduction and Developing a Closing in addition to giving an effective verbal and non-verbal greeting and good-bye, you will make a strong and positive first and last impression on your audience.

Humor

Humor is another powerful skill you can use to energize your presentation. Humor can create a good feeling. Humor encourages careful listening, builds rapport, and helps to make your audience remember your ideas. It also gives your audience a breather, a moment of relaxation during your presentation. Depending on your audience analysis, determine the amount and kind of humor that is appropriate.

☞ Point of Interest

Consider the following when incorporating humor into your presentation.

- ❏ Relate the humor to the topic being discussed.
- ❏ Use humor that fits you, that is comfortable for you, and that reflects your style.
- ❏ Use humorous stories and jokes that your audience will like and understand. Make sure you are confident and comfortable when telling the story.
- ❏ Make the joke or story a surprise; do not warn your audience that a joke is coming.
- ❏ Practice telling the joke or story before your presentation.
- ❏ Do not tell inappropriate jokes or stories. Unsuitable jokes and stories will destroy a presentation. It is a good idea to avoid jokes about religion, ethnicity, gender, and politics. Your audience analysis will determine if there are other topics you should avoid. If you have any doubts about using humor, leave it out of your presentation.
- ❏ Do tell humorous stories about yourself, if you can tie them into your presentation. Most people are comfortable telling stories about themselves, and it helps to establish rapport with the audience.
- ❏ Avoid using sarcasm in your presentation. Even though you may think that sarcasm could be used effectively, it tends to create uneasiness in your audience and conveys a negative impression of you.
- ❏ If you are not comfortable telling jokes or stories, you can also effectively use humor by using cartoons on overheads, flip charts, or slides. These cartoons can have the same positive impact as a joke or story; just make sure the cartoon is relevant to your presentation.
- ❏ Relax—humor is supposed to be fun—and remember you are giving a presentation to deliver a message; humor is a tool to help you.

We have discussed how verbal and non-verbal skills contribute to an effective presentation. Another important skill to develop is the effective use of notes.

Use of Notes

Many presenters feel more secure when using notes. However, relying on notes interferes with communicating your message effectively. The use of notes decreases your credibility because you look unprepared. Also, the constant motion of a presenter's eyes from the audience to the notes is annoying. As a result, the audience will pay more attention to the distracting movement than to what you are saying.

If you have your presentation written out in front of you, you will have a tendency to begin to read the presentation, even if you are well prepared. Reading a presentation, even for a few seconds, will cause you to lose the audience's attention and you may not ever get it back.

An alternative to using notes is to place your presentation outline on a slide or flip chart. This will give you confidence and also provide the audience a framework of your presentation that they can follow. Both you and your audience will be able to look at the outline together; therefore, eliminating the distraction of you reading your notes.

To prepare your outline, convert your presentation into bullet points. List only key words or phrases that emphasize important issues or facts and that will trigger the ideas you want to develop. An outline not only helps the audience to follow your presentation but also will assist you when preparing for the presentation.

Point of Interest

- ❑ All effective speakers have one thing in common—they TALK to their audience, they don't read to their audience.

- ❑ Have you ever been read to during a presentation? It is boring! If your material needs to be read, let the audience read it, put the information in their mailbox.

Reducing Stage Fright

For many people the prospect of delivering a presentation generates fear and apprehension. However, effective presenters give the impression that they are comfortable, confident, in control, and enjoying themselves. How do they do this?

Remember, presenting is a skill—a skill that anyone can learn. The best way to learn a skill is to practice, practice, and practice some more because the best antidote to stage fright is practice. The most effective way to gain control of stage fright is to take advantage of the confidence that comes from preparation and rehearsal. Stage fright decreases in direct proportion to the amount of preparation and practice.

When practicing, use positive visualization—rehearse your presentation in your mind. Imagine yourself presenting the content, imagine yourself presenting it well, and imagine your audience reacting positively. What we fill our mind with often becomes a self-fulfilling prophecy. Therefore, it is important to visualize yourself presenting successfully.

Everyone has some degree of stage fright when facing an audience. The issue becomes one of whether you use this nervous energy positively or negatively. Most seasoned performers and presenters will acknowledge that some degree of stage fright is beneficial. The adrenaline created before making a presentation can be channeled into positive energy resulting in an enthusiastic presentation.

Stage fright, however, can be negative when you allow it to take control of you instead of you controlling it. Stage fright controls you when you dwell on what you cannot do. "I know I will forget to mention the statistics." You control stage fright when you concentrate on what you can do. "I will mention the statistics following my introduction." Repeat this over and over as you are practicing, "I am a good presenter, I am a really good presenter." This will result in more self-confidence and a more positive attitude.

To avoid the vocal symptoms of nervousness, practice some presentation exercises to relax your voice and heavy breathing. Use deep breathing to ease your nerves. Inhale to a count of ten and then exhale to a count of ten. Concentrate on expanding and contracting your diaphragm rather than your chest.

In addition, drink warm clear liquids to relax your vocal chords. Avoid drinking dairy products as they coat your vocal chords and tongue leaving you with cottonmouth. Furthermore, avoid caffeine if you feel anxiety prior to presenting.

An all too common fault of presenters is that they do not rehearse as much as they should. Take advantage of these rehearsal guidelines and the other delivery techniques discussed.

☞ Point of Interest

There are several things to concentrate on when rehearsing your presentation.

- ❑ Familiarize yourself with the room in which you will be presenting.

- ❑ Familiarize yourself with any equipment you will be using so you can operate it without difficulty.

- ❑ Practice integrating your visual aids with your presentation and using them naturally so the presentation flows smoothly.

- ❑ Develop your ability to stand and move around in a natural manner.

- ❑ Look for flaws or gaps in your outline.

- ❑ Time your presentation to accommodate the time allowed.

- ❑ Practice with someone so you can rehearse maintaining eye contact.

- ❑ Tape record or videotape your presentation. Videotaping your presentation is the single best tool you can use to improve your presentation skills. As the saying goes, "the camera does not lie." Seeing and hearing yourself on videotape will help you to analyze your voice quality, rate, pitch, volume, and the number of times you use non-words, such as "ahhh" and "uhmm," or annoying phrases, such as "you know." Also, by taping your presentation you will notice any annoying gestures, movements, and mannerisms.

Also, do not discount the fact that when you have defined your purpose, analyzed your audience, organized your material, incorporated a transitional plan, and planned for an opening and closing, your presentation will be more effective. This preparation will diminish your stage fright, increase your self-confidence, reinforce credibility, and elevate your chances for success.

Use the presentation checklists on pages 108–112 to analyze your rehearsals. This will help you to identify areas for improvement.

Phase Four: Delivering the Presentation Summary

Effective Presenters Are Made, Not Born!

Great presenters develop their presentation skills by following the guidelines discussed in each of the Delivering the Presentation building blocks:

1 *Verbal Skills*

1 2 *Non-verbal Skills*

1 2 3 *Presentation Style*

By following these guidelines and by practicing your presentation you will develop your presentation skills and become a powerful and memorable presenter.

Phase Four: Delivering the Presentation Checklist

Word Usage

- ☐ Did you use conversational language?
- ☐ Did you use short words and sentences?
- ☐ Did you give specific examples and/or use analogies where appropriate?
- ☐ Did you eliminate all non-words and filler phrases?

Vocals

- ☐ Did you correctly pronounce all words?
- ☐ Did you use varied speech inflections?
- ☐ Was your tone objective and neutral?
- ☐ Did you vary your speaking rate?
- ☐ Did you slow down your speaking rate to emphasize main ideas?
- ☐ Did you project your voice so everyone could hear you?

(continued)

Phase Four: Delivering the Presentation Checklist *(continued)*

Body

- ❑ Was your posture dignified and relaxed?
- ❑ Did you comfortably use hand gestures?
- ❑ Did you avoid distracting gestures?
- ❑ Did you make eye contact with individuals throughout the audience?
- ❑ Did you smile at your audience?

Style

- ❑ Did you include a verbal and non-verbal hello?
- ❑ Did you include a verbal and non-verbal goodbye?
- ❑ Did you present from an outline instead of notes?
- ❑ Did you practice your presentation using a videotape or tape recorder?
- ❑ Did you practice positive visualization?
- ❑ Did you familiarize yourself with all of your equipment?
- ❑ Did you practice how to stand and move during your presentation?
- ❑ Did your presentation fit the time allowed?

Humor

- ❑ Was the humor, if used, appropriate and effective?

Phase Four: Effective Presentation Checklist

After you have viewed your presentation practice session on videotape, ask yourself these questions about your effectiveness as a presenter.

Opening

- ❑ Did you include a pleasant verbal and non-verbal greeting?
- ❑ Did you include an attention getter?
- ❑ Did you state a clear and concise purpose?
- ❑ Did you provide the necessary background?
- ❑ Did you state a plan of presentation for the presentation?

Body

- ❑ Did you limit your presentation to three to five main ideas?
- ❑ Did you incorporate a thorough transitional plan?
  - ❑ Did you state a lead-in at the beginning of each new section?
  - ❑ Did you provide connecting statements?
  - ❑ Did you summarize each section?
  - ❑ Did you use transitional statements between sections?

(continued)

Phase Four: Effective Presentation Checklist *(continued)*

Delivery

- ❑ Did you speak loud enough?
- ❑ Did you speak clearly?
- ❑ Did you maintain eye contact throughout the presentation?
- ❑ Did you establish eye contact with everyone in the audience?
- ❑ Did you smile throughout the presentation?
- ❑ Did you stand up straight?
- ❑ Did you use natural and appropriate gestures?
- ❑ Did you use specific, image-building words?
- ❑ Did you avoid using technical jargon?
- ❑ Did you avoid using non-words, such as "uh" and "uhm"?

Style

- ❑ Did you project enthusiasm?
- ❑ If you incorporated humor, was it effective?
  - ❑ Was the humor related to the topic?
  - ❑ Was the humor enjoyed by all?
- ❑ Did you appear comfortable?
- ❑ Did you appear confident?

(continued)

Phase Four: Effective Presentation Checklist *(continued)*

Use of Audiovisuals

❑ Were the visuals prepared correctly?

❑ Was only one concept per visual illustrated?

❑ Did you summarize the concept in words?

❑ Was the color used meaningful and effective?

❑ Did you effectively manipulate the visuals?

Closing

❑ Did you summarize the entire presentation?

❑ Did you clearly state evaluations, conclusions, recommendations, and/or actions desired?

❑ Did you provide a verbal and non-verbal goodbye?

Questions and Answers

❑ Did you indicate a Q & A process?

❑ Did you encourage questions?

❑ Did you repeat questions before answering them?

❑ Did you provide a close to the Q & A session?

Phase Four: Presentation Challenge

Videotape a mock presentation. Enlist a mentor or supervisor to watch the tape and complete the **Phase Four: Delivering the Presentation Checklist**. Ask this person to then review the checklist with you so they can elaborate on the critique.

APPENDIX:
ADDITIONAL PLANNING GUIDES

Phase Two: Introduction Planning Guide

Presentation Purpose _____

_____

I. Introduction

Attention Getter _____

_____

_____

_____

Background _____

_____

_____

_____

Scope _____

_____

_____

_____

Terms to Define_____

_____

_____

Plan of Presentation _____

_____

_____

_____

Phase Two: Developing the Body Planning Guide

Purpose _____

_____

First Main Idea _____

    Lead-in _____

    Support _____

    _____

    Support _____

    _____

    Support _____

    _____

    Support _____

    _____

    Summary _____

    _____

    Transition _____

    _____

(continued)

Phase Two: Developing the Body
Planning Guide *(continued)*

Second Main Idea _____

    Lead-in_____

    Support _____

    _____

    Support _____

    _____

    Support _____

    _____

    Support _____

    _____

    Summary _____

    _____

    Transition _____

    _____

(continued)

Phase Two: Developing the Body Planning Guide *(continued)*

Third Main Idea _____

    Lead-in_____

    Support _____

    _____

    Support _____

    _____

    Support _____

    _____

    Support _____

    _____

    Summary _____

    _____

    Transition _____

    _____

(continued)

Phase Two: Developing the Body
Planning Guide *(continued)*

Fourth Main Idea _____

    Lead-in_____

    Support _____

    _____

    Support _____

    _____

    Support _____

    _____

    Support _____

    _____

    Summary _____

    _____

    _____

    _____